SESAME STREET

food Crafts

First published by Parragon in 2009

Parragon
Queen Street House
4 Queen Street
Bath BA1 1HE, UK

ISBN 978-1-4075-7199-7

Printed in China

123 SESAME STREET®

food Crafts

PaRragon

Bath New York Singapore Hong Kong Cologne Delhi Melbourne

TIPS FOR SUCCESS

Prepare your space

Cover your workspace with newspaper or a plastic or paper tablecloth. Make sure you and your children are wearing clothes (including shoes!) that you don't mind becoming spattered with food, paint, or glue. But relax! You'll never completely avoid mess; in fact, it's part of the fun!

Wash your hands

Wash your hands (and your child's hands) before starting a new project, and clean up as you go along. Clean hands make for clean crafts! Remember to wash your hands afterward, too, using soap and warm water to get off any of the remaining materials.

Follow steps carefully

Follow each step carefully, and in the sequence in which it appears. We've tested all the projects; we know they work, and we want them to work for you, too. Also, ask your children, if they are old enough, to read along with you as you work through the steps. For a younger child, you can direct her to look at the pictures on the page to try to guess what the next step is.

Measure precisely

If a project gives you measurements, use your ruler, T-square, measuring cups, or measuring spoons to make sure you measure as accurately as you can. Sometimes the success of the project may depend on it. Also, this is a great opportunity to teach measuring techniques to your child.

Be patient

You may need to wait while something bakes or leave paint, glue, or clay to dry, sometimes for a few hours or even overnight. Encourage your child to be patient as well; explain to her why she must wait, and, if possible, find ways to entertain her as you are waiting. For example you can show her how long you have to wait by pointing out the time on a clock.

Clean up

When you've finished your project, clean up any mess. Store all the materials together so that they are ready for the next time you want to craft. Ask your child to help.

Bread dough animals

Elmo loves the smell of fresh baked bread. Uncooked bread is called dough. It's easy to make shapes with bread dough, like these animal shapes.

You will need

- Mixing bowl
- 1 packet active dry yeast
- ⅔ cup warm water
- 1 teaspoon salt
- 1 teaspoon sugar
- ¼ cup unsalted butter
- 1 cup flour
- Raisins

1

In a mixing bowl, dissolve the yeast in the warm water. Stir in the salt and sugar, then add the flour and butter.

Kids 2

With your hands, make a ball with the dough and knead it for 5 minutes, or until the dough feels smooth and stretchy.

Divide the dough into 3 or 4 smaller pieces and shape into animals, such as a snail, a turtle, a fish, and a snake. Push raisins into the dough for eyes.

Place the animal shapes onto a baking sheet, then leave the dough to rise in a warm place for 30 minutes. Bake in the oven for 20 minutes at 350°F until golden in color. Leave to cool, then enjoy your tasty animal snacks.

Snails and turtles have hard shells. Can you think of any other creatures that have shells?

CRUNCHY SALADS

YOU WILL NEED

- Jar
- Saucer
- Marker pen
- Piece of cheesecloth
- Scissors
- Elastic rubber band
- Spoon
- Mung beans or other seeds for sprouting

Choose a pretty-shaped jar, then wash and dry it thoroughly. Draw around the saucer on the cheesecloth. Make sure the circle is a few inches bigger all round than the top of the jar.

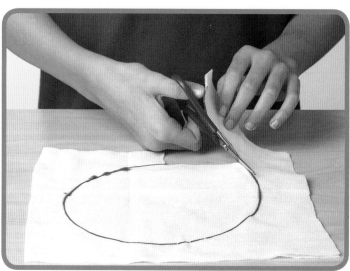

Cut out the circle with scissors. This will be the lid for the jar. You will need an elastic rubber band to hold the fabric in place on top of the jar.

Place a large spoonful of mung beans (or other seeds) in the jar. Cover with water and leave to soak for two hours. Strain away the water.

4

Put the lid on the jar. Wash the spouts with water three times a day and watch them grow. When they are long enough to eat (before the leaves appear) wash them thoroughly. Use them in salads for a crunchy, fresh taste!

DID YOU KNOW? Sprouted seeds are very healthy. They are packed full of vitamins.

Try sprouting alfalfa or sunflower seeds – but don't use garden seeds, which may have been sprayed with chemicals.

Choc chunk cookies

**Me hear you say the word "cookie."
Can me make these delicious cookies
with you?**

You will need
- Large mixing bowl
- Sieve
- 2¼ cups all-purpose flour
- Pinch of salt
- 1 teaspoon baking powder
- 1 tablespoon butter
- ¾ cup light brown sugar
- 2 eggs, beaten
- 2 ounces corn syrup
- 3 ounces semi-sweet chocolate
- Rolling pin
- A cookie cutter
- Nonstick cooking spray
- Baking sheet

1

Pre-heat the oven to 325°F. Sift the flour, salt, and baking powder into a large bowl.

kids 2

With your fingers, rub the butter into the dry ingredients. Add the sugar. In a cup, stir together the eggs and the corn syrup.

kids 3

With a wooden spoon, beat the ingredients until they are thoroughly combined. Break the chocolate into small chunks and add to the mixture.

Place the dough on a board. Sprinkle it lightly with flour so it doesn't stick to the rolling pin. Roll out the dough until it's about ½-inch thick. With a cookie cutter, cut out the cookies, like these star-shaped cookies.

Lightly grease a baking sheet with nonstick cooking spray or vegetable oil. Place the cookies about 2 inches apart on the baking sheet. Bake for about 15 minutes, until golden.

After me eat cookie, me have apple! Oh me so proud!

Fruit smoothies

Me love smoothies almost as much as cookies! M-M-M-M-M!

You will need

For a strawberry and mango smoothie:
- 4 strawberries
- ¾ cup sliced mango
- 1 small banana
- Juice of 1 orange
- 3 tablespoons low fat yogurt
- 1 tablespoon honey
- Blender container
- Glass and straws

kids 1

Chop three strawberries, the mango, and the banana. Put them in the bowl of the blender with all the other ingredients.

2

Blend everything until you have a smooth, thick mixture.

kids 3

Pour the smoothie into a glass. Cut the remaining strawberry in half and use it to decorate the glass. Add straws.

Elmo loves smoothies. You can make them with pineapple, blueberries, peaches, or lots of other fruit you like!

It is very hot in Mexico so we eat Popsicles to keep cool. Why not make a fruit Popsicle using your smoothie? Just pour the mixture into a tray, add a Popsicle stick, and put it in the freezer!

Pasta jewelry

Now me making pasta jewelry with Zoe. You can use these shapes and colors, or choose your own.

1

Paint the pasta wheels in green, blue, and purple acrylic paint, or any colors you like.

You will need

- Dried pasta shapes: 6 wheels, 24 curly macaroni
- Acrylic paints: green, blue, purple, gold
- Lump of modeling clay
- Toothpicks
- Colored string, elastic, or cord

Tie a button to the string while you thread the shapes to keep them from falling off!

2

Paint the macaroni gold, and put all the shapes on the ends of toothpicks stuck into a large piece of modeling clay.

3

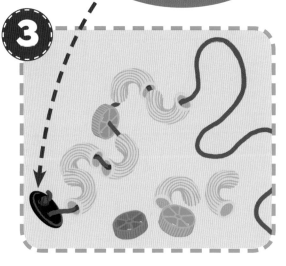

Thread three macaronis then a wheel onto the colored string or cord. Repeat this until all the pasta is threaded.

4

Knot the two ends of the string together, making sure you have made your necklace big enough to go over your head.

There are a lot of different pasta shapes, like wheels or bowties. Which one is your favorite?

FRUIT POPSICLES

YOU WILL NEED

- Popsicle molds or paper cups
- Fruit juices
- Popsicle sticks
- Chopped fruit (small pieces)
- Sprinkles

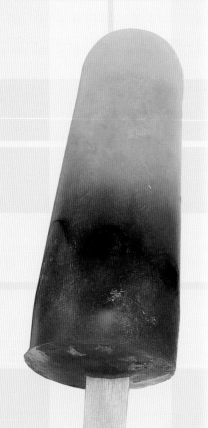

1
KIDS

Choose your favorite juices and carefully pour them into the Popsicle molds so they are half full.

2
KIDS

Put the molds in the freezer until the juice is starting to set, but isn't completely frozen. Now place the Popsicle sticks into the molds. Add some chopped fruit and top up with different flavored juices. Put the Popsicles back into the freezer to set.

③

When they are completely frozen, run the molds under a warm tap to help loosen the Popsicles before removing them.

DID YOU KNOW?
Before freezers were invented, ice was a luxury!

For a special treat, add sprinkles at the bottom of the mold.

Gingerbread men

This no cookie. Me and Ernie making gingerbread cookie to eat. Ya-ya.

You will need

To make 10 gingerbread men:
- 2 tablespoons butter
- ½ cup brown sugar
- ¼ cup (4 tablespoons) molasses
- 1 cup plus 2 tablespoons all-purpose flour
- Pinch of salt
- ½ teaspoon each: baking powder, ginger, cinnamon
- Gingerbread man cutter
- Rolling pin, baking sheet, sieve, bowl, saucepan
- Frosting: ½ cup confectioner's sugar, water, blue food coloring, plastic sandwich bag

Heat the butter, molasses, and sugar gently in a pan until the sugar dissolves and the butter melts.

Sift together the flour, salt, baking powder, ginger, and cinnamon into a large bowl. Add the sugar mixture, and with a wooden spoon, mix well.

kids

Form the dough into a ball, wrap it in plastic wrap, and refrigerate for at least an hour. Then, roll the dough out to about ½-inch thick.

18

4

Pre-heat oven to 350°F. Grease a baking sheet. Using the cutter, cut out the cookies. Place them 2-inches apart on a baking sheet; bake for 8-12 minutes, depending upon size of the cookies. Let cool.

5

To make the frosting: sift the confectioner's sugar into a bowl, add a few drops of food coloring, and a little water. Mix until the frosting is thick but still a bit runny.

6

Make a pastry bag by snipping the corner off a plastic sandwich bag, then spooning the frosting into the top. Gently squeeze the frosting onto the cookies.

You can make gingerbread boys by using a smaller cookie cutter. Make gingerbread ladies and girls, too!

Fishy burgers

Me LOVE cookies but me like fishy burgers, too. Do you like burgers or cookies or BOTH?

You will need

To make 4 burgers:
- Vegetable oil
- 1 small onion, chopped
- 1 teaspoon chopped parsley (or herb of choice)
- ½ cup breadcrumbs
- 8-ounce can red salmon or tuna packed with water
- 1 egg
- Salt and pepper to taste
- Flour
- Lettuce, tomato slices, onion rings, mayonnaise
- 4 wholewheat burger buns
- Skillet

kids 1

Heat 2 teaspoonfuls of oil in the skillet; add the onion, herbs, and breadcrumbs and saute gently for 5 minutes.

kids 2

Pour the mixture into a bowl and let cool. Add the fish, egg, salt, and pepper. Mix everything together with your hands.

kids 3

Sprinkle some flour onto the work surface and shape the mixture into burgers.

Wash and dry the skillet, add oil, and place over medium heat. Fry the burger for 5 minutes on each side.

Put each burger on a bun and garnish with lettuce, tomato slices, onion rings, and mayonnaise.

It says here that you can use tuna instead of salmon. The smellier, the better, I say!

Tasty cupcakes

A cupcake is almost as good as cookie. Me have fun making them and me have even more fun eating them.

1

Mix the butter and sugar in a large bowl. Mix in the egg a little at a time. Add a few drops of vanilla extract.

You will need

To make 12 cakes:
- ¼ cup butter
- Heaped ¼ cup sugar
- 1 egg, beaten
- Vanilla extract
- ¾ cup self-rising flour
- Foil mini bake cups
- Wooden spoon, dessert spoon, cookie sheet, sieve, and cooling rack

For the frosting:
- ½ cup confectioner's sugar
- Few drops red food coloring
- Metallic cake decorations
- Butter knife and butter

kids 2

Sift the flour into the bowl. Using a wooden spoon, mix it in gently to make a batter.

kids 3

Pre-heat the oven to 400°F. Place 2 tablespoons of batter into each cup. Put them on a cookie sheet and bake for 10 minutes. Let them cool.

4

To make the frosting, sift the confectioner's sugar into a bowl. Add a few drops of food coloring and just enough water to make a paste.

5

Spread the frosting onto the cakes. Sprinkle metallic balls or other decorations on top and let the frosting set.

The word "cupcake" starts with the letter C. Think of some other foods that start with the letter C.

LUNCHBOXES

YOU WILL NEED

- Plastic food storage box with lid or lunchbox
- Craft foam
- Scissors
- Foam letters
- White glue or sticky foam pads
- Double-sided tap (optional)

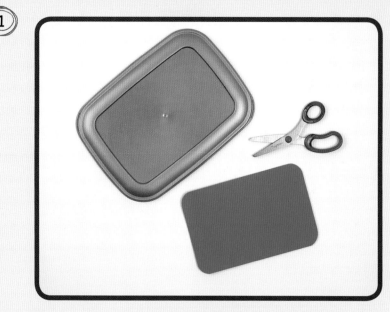

① Cut out a rectangle of foam to fit onto the lunch box or lid of the plastic box. Round off the corners to make it look neat.

②

Cut out foam shapes to decorate the foam rectangle. Arrange them with some ready-cut foam letters to spell out your name. Experiment with positioning, until you are happy with your design, then glue it in place.

③
KIDS

Place the finished design onto the lid. You can use glue, but if you use sticky foam pads or double-sided tape it can easily be removed for washing or switched for another design.

DID YOU KNOW?
The world's biggest pre-packed sandwich was eight feet two inches long!

Cut out shapes of your favorite foods to decorate the lid.

Peppermint candies

Me needs help making these scrumptious sweets, but me needs no help eating them!

You will need

To make 20 candies:
- 4 cups confectioner's sugar
- 1 egg white
- Juice of half a lemon
- A few drops of peppermint extract
- Green food coloring
- Bar of semi-sweet chocolate
- Sieve, bowl, cookie cutter, wooden spoon, saucepan

kids 1

Sift the confectioner's sugar into a large mixing bowl.

2

Separate the egg yolk from the white. Add the egg white to the confectioner's sugar.

kids 3

With your hands or a spoon, mix it together until you have made a soft lump. Add the lemon juice, peppermint extract, and food coloring.

Pour the lump onto a cold surface and flatten it to about ½ inch thick. With a cookie cutter, cut out the shapes, put them on a baking sheet, and leave them in a cool, dry place to set for around 30 minutes.

Break up the bar of chocolate and put it in a bowl. Put the bowl over a saucepan of simmering water and stir the chocolate until it has melted.

6

Take the bowl off the heat and quickly dip half of each candy into the chocolate. Leave the candies until the chocolate hardens.

You could make fruit chocs instead. Dip strawberries, cherries, and sliced apple in the melted chocolate. Phew! All this dipping can make a monster dizzy.

Banana sundae

Me tummy full. But me want to try this banana sundae. The other fruit sundaes look yummy, too!

You will need

- Vanilla ice cream
- 1 banana
- Chocolate sauce
- Candy sprinkles
- Sundae glass and spoon

1 Spoon ice cream into the bottom of a sundae dish.

2 Add a layer of sliced banana and some chocolate sauce. Then add more ice cream. Repeat the layers until you have only 3 slices of banana left.

3 Decorate the top of the sundae with the banana slices, some additional chocolate sauce, and the sprinkles.

Fresh strawberries and raspberry ripple ice cream make a tasty fruity sundae.

This delicious sundae is made with peach ice cream, peach slices, and crushed meringue.

TREAT TIME!

YOU WILL NEED

- 4 carrots, peeled
- 2 zucchini
- 4 stalks celery
- Half a cucumber
- 1 red bell pepper
- 1 yellow bell pepper
- 8 baby corns
- 1 cup low-fat cream cheese
- 2 tablespoons milk
- 2 scallions, finely chopped
- 1 tablespoon parsley
- 1 tablespoon chives
- Salt and pepper

1

Cut the carrots, zucchini, and celery into sticks two inches long. Halve the cucumber, remove the seeds, and cut into equal-sized sticks.

2

Halve the peppers and remove the seeds. Cut each into long strips.

Make the cheesy dip by mixing the cream cheese and milk until smooth. Add the other ingredients, season with salt and pepper to taste, and stir until well mixed. Now it's ready to enjoy with your tasty, crunchy treats.

DID YOU KNOW? The biggest cucumber ever grown was over 31 inches long.

Blue furry monsters love vegetables!

INDEX